# Gin is good for you

A comical collection of quotes for gin devotees

ISBN: 978-1-912511-04-4

Created by Reckless Indiscretions
Images under license from Shuttertock

BELL & MACKENZIE
PUBLISHING LIMITED
www.bellmackenzie.com

*To Gin or not*

*to Gin...*

*silly question*

When life
**hands you lemons**

make a

# GIN & TONIC

Forgive me father
for I have Ginned

**IT'S NEVER**

# TOO EARLY

## FOR

### GIN O' CLOCK

_____

*Gym?
I thought you said
Gin!*

_____

# Don't cry
## OVER SPILT MILK
it could

# have been
# GIN

Home
is where the Gin is

I'M IN A GIN-TASTIC MOOD TODAY

**GOOD FRIENDS**
OFFER ADVICE
REAL FRIENDS
OFFER GIN

The best tonic has a
large Gin
in it

*Gin,*

*because everyone*

*needs a hobby*

Step aside

coffee

this is a job for

GIN

Life is full of miracles
Gin is just one of them

There is nothing *better than a*

*friend*

*unless it is a*

friend

with Gin

*This house runs better on love, laughter and Gin*

Life is too short for single Gins

# I NEVER DRINK

ANYTHING STRONGER THAN

# GIN

BEFORE BREAKFAST

*Keep calm*

*and drink*

*Gin & tonic*

Gin.
Do more of what makes you happy.

# Gin.
## It's always the right thing to do.

*Gin*

*is liquid sanity*

If you can't remember my

# name

just say

## Gin

and I'll turn

# AROUND

A yawn
is a silent scream for Gin

# A CUP OF

~~TEA~~

GIN

SOLVES EVERYTHING

_I want someone to look at me the same way I look at Gin._

Education is important
But Gin is importanter

I cut down Gin and
tonic by half
Now I just drink the

# Gin

*You should have a warm heart and a cold Gin and tonic*

# Gin
# lovers
## make better
# LOVERS

Water is composed of two gins,
Oxygin and Hydrogin.
Oxygin is pure Gin. Hydrogin
is Gin and water.

# TRUST ME
# YOU CAN
# DANCE
# SAID GIN

# A PERFECT MARTINI

SHOULD BE MADE
BY FILLING A GLASS

WITH GIN

THEN WAVING IT IN THE GENERAL DIRECTION OF

ITALY

Noel Coward

Ashes to ashes,
dust to dust.
When life's a bitch,
Gin is a must.

*Spilling your Gin is the adult equivalent to losing a balloon*

If at first you don't succeed, try, try a Gin

# I
# AM
# GIN-VINCIBLE

# THERE'S A TIME
## AND A PLACE
# FOR GIN
## IN MY HAND AND NOW!

I don't know what reception I'm at, but for God's sake give me a Gin and tonic

Dennis Thatcher

_Nobody is perfect but if you drink Gin you're pretty close!_

# Exercise is
## walking round the house
looking

for my
glass of

# GIN

More Gin.  More Grins.

A GIN AND TONIC HAS
**91 CALORIES**
A BANANA HAS
**115 CALORIES**

# Life Happens Gin Helps

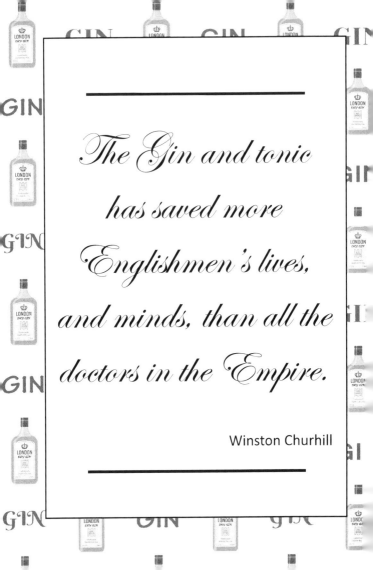

The Gin and tonic has saved more Englishmen's lives, and minds, than all the doctors in the Empire.

Winston Churhill

Printed in Great Britain
by Amazon